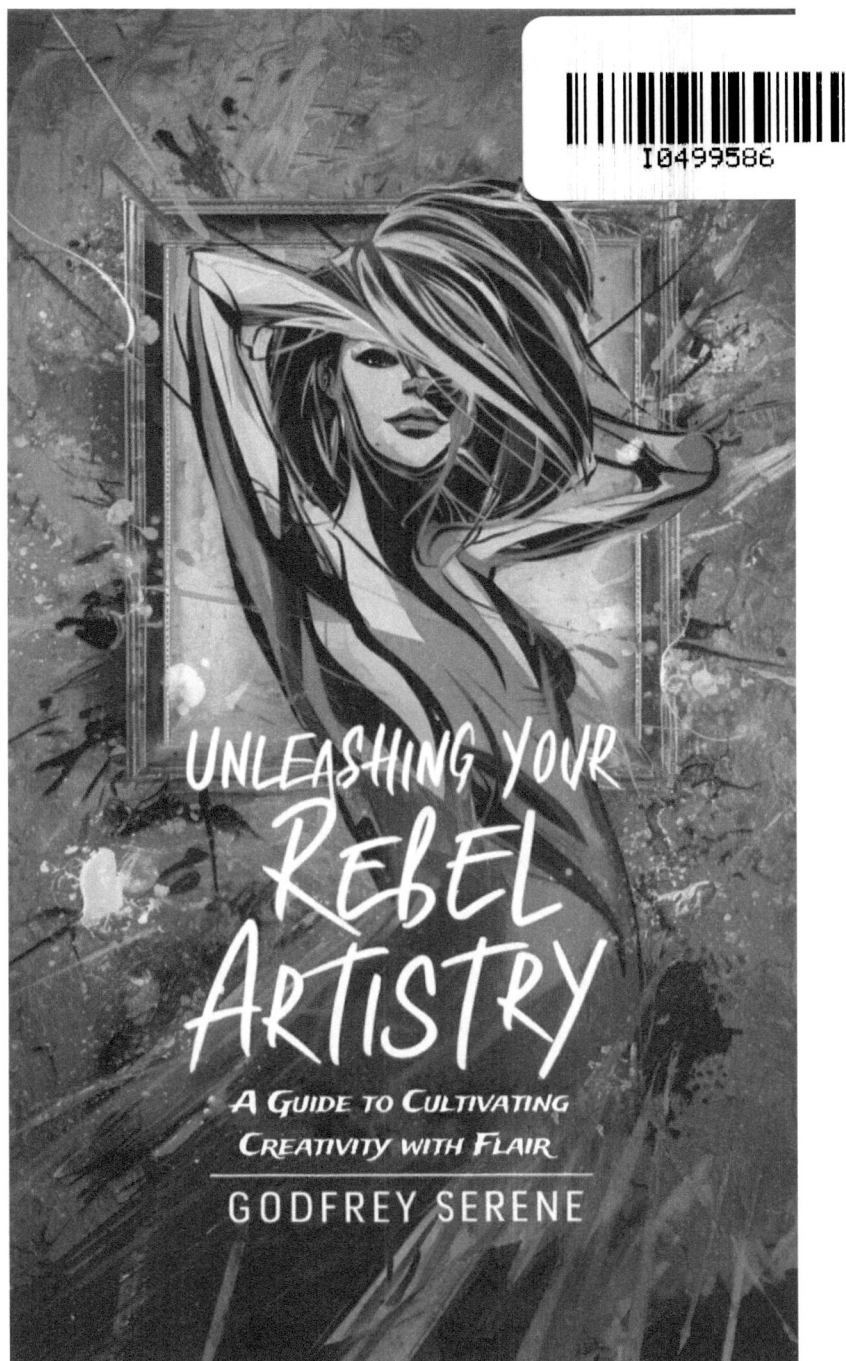

MR.GODFREYSERENE

UNLEASHING YOUR REBEL ARTISTRY:
A GUIDE TO CULTIVATING CREATIVITY WITH FLAIR

Godfrey Serene

TABLE OF CONTENTS:

Introduction: Embracing Your Rebel Spirit

Chapter 1: The Power of Authentic Expression
Chapter 2: Channelling Your Inner Rebel
Chapter 3: Breaking the Rules, Making Your Mark
Chapter 4: Finding Inspiration in Unconventional Places
Chapter 5: Embracing Imperfection as Perfection
Chapter 6: Navigating Criticism with Confidence
Chapter 7: The Art of Risk-Taking
Chapter 8: Cultivating a Unique Artistic Voice
Chapter 9: Honing Your Craft with Passion and Persistence
Chapter 10: Balancing Tradition with Innovation
Chapter 11: Creating Impactful Art That Challenges the Status Quo
Chapter 12: Overcoming Creative Blocks with Rebellion
Chapter 13: Building a Community of Fellow Rebels
Chapter 14: Embracing Change and Adaptation
Chapter 15: Making Your Art Matter: Advocacy and Activism
Conclusion: Embracing Your Rebel Artistry Journey

About the Author
Acknowledgments

Introduction: Embracing Your Rebel Spirit

"Unleashing Your Rebel Artistry," where we celebrate the power of creative rebellion. In this guide, we'll explore how to infuse your art with a rebel touch, pushing boundaries, challenging norms, and forging your own path in the world of creativity. Whether you're a seasoned artist looking to reignite your rebellious spark or a budding creator eager to break free from convention, this book is for you. Let's embark on this exhilarating journey together and unleash the full potential of your artistic rebellion.

CHAPTER 1: THE POWER OF AUTHENTIC EXPRESSION

In the realm of art, authenticity reigns supreme. It's the cornerstone upon which all meaningful creative endeavours are built. Authentic expression isn't just about creating pretty pictures or catchy tunes—it's about baring your soul, sharing your truth, and connecting with others on a deeper level. In this chapter, we'll explore why authenticity is essential for any rebel artist and discover practical techniques for embracing your true self in your creative work.

Embracing Your Unique Perspective

Every artist sees the world through their own lens—a lens shaped by their experiences, beliefs, and values. Your perspective is what sets you apart from everyone else, and it's what gives your art its distinct flavour. Instead of trying to mimic the style of others or conforming to societal expectations, embrace what makes you different. Celebrate your quirks, your flaws, and your idiosyn

crasies. These are the things that make your art uniquely yours.

Honouring Your Truth

Authentic expression requires honesty—both with yourself and with your audience. It's about being unapologetically true to who you are and what you believe in. Don't be afraid to explore the depths of your emotions, even if it means confronting uncomfortable truths. Your art is a reflection of your innermost thoughts and feelings, so let it speak honestly and authentically.

Cultivating Self-Awareness

To truly express yourself authentically, you must first understand who you are as an artist. Take the time to explore your strengths, your weaknesses, and your creative impulses. Reflect on what motivates you, what inspires you, and what drives you to create. The more self-aware you become, the easier it will be to channel your authentic voice into your art.

Finding Your Voice

Your artistic voice is the essence of who you are as a creator—it's what sets your work apart and makes it unmistakably yours. Finding your voice is a journey of self-discovery, experimentation, and growth. It's about exploring different mediums, styles, and techniques until you find the perfect fit for your unique perspective. Don't be afraid to take risks, make mistakes, and push the boundaries of your creativity. Your voice is waiting to be heard—so let it roar.

Conclusion

Authentic expression is the lifeblood of rebel artistry. It's what fuels our creativity, drives our passion, and sets our work apart from the rest. By embracing our unique perspective, honouring our truth, cultivating self-awareness, and finding our voice, we can unleash the full power of our artistic rebellion. So go forth, fellow rebel artists, and let your authenticity shine bright. The world is waiting for your truth.

CHAPTER 2: CHANNELLING YOUR INNER REBEL

Within the heart of every artist lies a dormant rebel, waiting for the moment to break free and disrupt the established norms of creativity. It's that voice inside that urges us to question, to challenge, and to dare to be different. In this chapter, we'll embark on a journey to awaken and harness the power of our inner rebel, transforming it into a driving force behind our artistic expression.

Embracing Unconventional Ideas

The first step in channelling our inner rebel is to embrace the unconventional. It's about daring to explore ideas that defy convention and push the boundaries of artistic expression. Instead of adhering to the tried and true, we must be willing to venture into uncharted territory, unafraid of the risks that come with innovation. Whether it's experimenting with new techniques, exploring alternative mediums, or challenging traditional artistic concepts, embracing the unconventional is key to unleashing our creative rebellion.

Defying Expectations

To truly channel our inner rebel, we must be willing to defy expectations. It's about refusing to be confined by the limitations imposed by others and daring to carve out our own path. Whether it's rejecting societal norms, challenging the expectations of our peers, or defying the conventions of our chosen medium, defying expectations is a hallmark of true artistic rebellion. By breaking free from the constraints of what is expected, we open ourselves up to new possibilities and pave the way for truly groundbreaking artistic expression.

Embracing Discomfort

Channelling our inner rebel often requires us to embrace discomfort. It's about stepping outside of our comfort zones and confronting the unknown with courage and determination. Whether it's tackling difficult subject matter, confronting our own fears and insecurities, or facing the judgment of others, embracing discomfort is essential to pushing the boundaries of our creativity. It's through discomfort that we grow, evolve, and ultimately, transcend the limitations of our own minds.

Finding Inspiration in the Unlikely

True rebels find inspiration in the most unlikely of places. It's about opening our minds to the world around us and finding beauty in the unconventional, the overlooked, and the unexpected. Whether it's drawing inspiration from the chaos of the city streets, the serenity of nature, or the raw emotions of the human experience, finding inspiration in the unlikely is a hallmark of true artistic rebellion. By looking beyond, the obvious, we can discover new avenues of creativity and unlock the full potential of our artistic vision.

Conclusion

Channelling your inner rebel is not just about creating art—it's about embracing a mindset of fearlessness, defiance, and unapologetic self-expression. It's about daring to challenge the status quo, to push the boundaries of what is possible, and to unleash the full power of your creative potential. So, embrace the unconventional, defy expectations, embrace discomfort, and find inspiration in the unlikely. For it is through rebellion that true artistry is born.

CHAPTER 3: BREAKING THE RULES, MAKING YOUR MARK

In the world of art, rules are meant to be broken. It's in the act of defiance, of shattering the constraints of tradition, that true innovation thrives. In this chapter, we'll delve into the exhilarating realm of rule-breaking and explore how daring to challenge conventions can propel your artistry to new heights.

Embracing Creative Freedom

The first step in breaking the rules is to embrace the freedom that comes with it. It's about liberating yourself from the confines of conventional thinking and giving yourself permission to explore the unknown. Whether it's experimenting with unconventional techniques, abandoning traditional artistic norms, or defying the expectations of others, embracing creative freedom is essential to making your mark as an artist.

Rejecting Limitations

Breaking the rules means rejecting limitations—both external and internal. It's about refusing to be bound by the constraints of what is considered "possible" or "acceptable" and daring to

push the boundaries of your creativity to the fullest extent. Whether it's challenging the limits of your chosen medium, defying the constraints of time and space, or transcending the boundaries of your own imagination, rejecting limitations is key to making your mark as an artist.

Embracing Imperfection

In the pursuit of artistic greatness, perfection is the enemy of progress. It's in the flaws, the imperfections, and the mistakes that true beauty often lies. By embracing imperfection, we free ourselves from the burden of unrealistic expectations and open ourselves up to the raw, unfiltered essence of creativity. Whether it's celebrating the beauty of a rough sketch, the spontaneity of a messy painting, or the authenticity of a flawed performance, embracing imperfection is essential to making your mark as an artist.

Taking Risks

Breaking the rules requires courage—the courage to take risks, to defy conventions, and to embrace uncertainty. It's about stepping outside of your comfort zone and daring to venture into the unknown, unafraid of the potential pitfalls that lie ahead. Whether it's embarking on a bold new artistic experiment, challenging the expectations of your audience, or risking failure in pursuit of greatness, taking risks is essential to making your mark as an artist.

Leaving Your Legacy

In the end, breaking the rules is about leaving your mark on the world—to create something that transcends the boundaries of time and space, something that resonates with others on a profound level, something that leaves a lasting legacy for generations to come. Whether it's through ground-breaking innovation, revolutionary ideas, or fearless self-expression, breaking the rules is your opportunity to make your mark on the world and leave behind a legacy that will inspire others for years to come.

Conclusion

In the journey of artistic expression, breaking the rules is not just an act of rebellion—it's an act of liberation, of self-discovery, and of profound creativity. So, embrace creative freedom, reject limitations, embrace imperfection, take risks, and leave your mark on the world. For it is in the daring defiance of convention that true artistic greatness is born.

CHAPTER 4: FINDING INSPIRATION IN UNCONVENTIONAL PLACES

In the vast landscape of creativity, inspiration can be found in the most unexpected of places. It's not always nestled within the confines of a pristine studio or hidden away in the pages of a revered art book. Instead, true inspiration often lurks in the shadows, waiting to be discovered in the unlikeliest of places. In this chapter, we'll embark on a journey to uncover the boundless wellsprings of creativity that lie beyond the beaten path and explore how venturing into the unknown can ignite the flames of artistic brilliance.

Embracing the Chaos of the Urban Jungle

The bustling streets of the city are a veritable treasure trove of inspiration, teeming with life, energy, and raw emotion. From the cacophony of honking horns to the kaleidoscope of colours that adorn graffiti-covered walls, the urban jungle is a feast for the senses. It's in the chaos of the city streets that we can find inspiration in the mundane, the ordinary, and the overlooked. Whether it's the rhythmic clatter of a passing subway train or the whispered conversations of strangers passing by, the city is a symphony of inspiration waiting to be explored.

Seeking Solace in the Serenity of Nature

In the tranquil embrace of nature, inspiration takes on a different hue—a softer, more introspective shade. From the gentle rustle of leaves in the breeze to the mesmerizing dance of sunlight on water, the natural world is a canvas upon which inspiration paints its most sublime masterpieces. It's in the serenity of a quiet forest glade or the vast expanse of a star-filled sky that we can find solace, renewal, and a deep connection to the world around us. Whether it's the vibrant hues of a sunset or the delicate beauty of a wildflower, nature is a wellspring of inspiration waiting to be tapped.

Exploring the Depths of the Human Psyche

Perhaps the most profound source of inspiration lies within the depths of the human psyche—a labyrinthine maze of thoughts, emotions, and experiences waiting to be explored. It's in the raw, unfiltered depths of our own minds that we can find the most profound insights, the most poignant truths, and the most stirring revelations. Whether it's delving into the recesses of our deepest fears or basking in the warmth of our most cherished memories, the human psyche is a vast reservoir of inspiration waiting to be plumbed.

Finding Beauty in the Mundane

Sometimes, inspiration can be found in the simplest of things—in the everyday moments that often pass us by unnoticed. It's in the mundane routines of life that we can find beauty, meaning, and purpose. Whether it's the warmth of a morning cup of coffee or the quiet companionship of a faithful pet, the mundane moments of life are imbued with a quiet grace that can inspire us to see the world in a new light. It's in the ordinary that we can find the extraordinary, if only we take the time to look.

Conclusion

In the quest for inspiration, there are no boundaries, no limits, and no rules. It's a journey of exploration, of discovery, and of wonder—a journey that can lead us to the most unexpected of places. So embrace the chaos of the urban jungle, seek solace in the serenity of nature, explore the depths of the human psyche, and find beauty in the mundane. For it is in the unlikeliest of places that true inspiration often lies, waiting to be discovered by those bold enough to venture

CHAPTER 5: EMBRACING IMPERFECTION AS PERFECTION

In a world obsessed with flawless beauty and impeccable precision, embracing imperfection may seem counterintuitive. Yet, within the realm of artistry, imperfection is not just accepted—it is celebrated as the very essence of creativity. In this chapter, we'll explore the profound beauty that lies within imperfection, and how embracing its inherent flaws can lead to the creation of art that resonates on a deeply human level.

The Flaws That Define Us

In a world where perfection is often equated with worthiness, it's easy to overlook the beauty that lies within our imperfections. Yet, it is our flaws—the cracks in the facade, the blemishes on the canvas—that make us truly unique. In art, as in life, it is often the imperfections that define us, that give depth and character to our creations. By embracing our flaws, we can tap into the raw, unfiltered essence of our humanity and create art that speaks to the soul.

The Beauty of the Unpredictable

In the pursuit of perfection, we often seek to control every aspect of our creative process—to meticulously plan every stroke of the brush, every note of the melody. Yet, it is in the moments of spontaneity, of chaos, that true magic often happens. By embracing imperfection, we open ourselves up to the beauty of the unpredictable, allowing ourselves to be swept away by the currents of inspiration and creativity. It is in the unexpected twists and turns of our artistic journey that we often find our most profound moments of clarity and insight.

Embracing the Process, Not Just the Outcome

In a culture that values instant gratification and immediate results, it's easy to lose sight of the true joy of creation—the journey itself. Yet, it is in the process of creation, in the act of bringing our visions to life, that we find our greatest fulfilment. By embracing imperfection, we can learn to appreciate the beauty of the journey—the mistakes, the setbacks, the moments of doubt—as much as the final destination. It is in the journey that we truly come to understand ourselves as artists, as creators, as human beings.

Finding Beauty in the Unfinished

In a world that values completeness and closure, there is a certain beauty in the unfinished—in the rough sketches, the half-formed ideas, the works-

in-progress. By embracing imperfection, we can learn to see the beauty in the incomplete, the potential in the unfinished. It is in the gaps, the spaces left to be filled, that our imaginations can run wild and our creativity can flourish. By embracing imperfection, we can learn to revel in the beauty of the journey, rather than fixating on the destination.

Conclusion

In the pursuit of artistic excellence, imperfection is not a flaw to be corrected—it is a gift to be cherished. By embracing imperfection, we can tap into the raw, unfiltered essence of our humanity, creating art that speaks to the soul and resonates with the heart. So embrace the flaws, celebrate the unpredictability, and revel in the beauty of the unfinished. For it is in imperfection that true perfection often lies.

CHAPTER 6: NAVIGATING CRITICISM WITH CONFIDENCE

Criticism is an inevitable part of the artistic journey, but it doesn't have to be a roadblock. In this chapter, we'll explore strategies for navigating criticism with confidence, turning feedback into fuel for growth, and embracing the transformative power of constructive critique.

Embracing the Growth Mindset

The first step in navigating criticism with confidence is to embrace a growth mindset. Instead of viewing criticism as a personal attack, see it as an opportunity for growth and improvement. Adopting a mindset that welcomes feedback, even when it's difficult to hear, allows you to approach criticism with an open heart and a willingness to learn.

Separating the Art from the Artist

Criticism can feel personal, but it's important to remember that it's not a reflection of your worth as an artist. Learn to separate your art from yourself, understanding that critique of your work is not a judgment of your value as a person. By detaching yourself emotionally from criticism,

you can approach it with a clear mind and a sense of perspective.

Seeking Out Constructive Feedback

Not all criticism is created equal. Learn to distinguish between constructive feedback, which is aimed at helping you improve, and destructive criticism, which serves only to tear you down. Surround yourself with trusted mentors, peers, and collaborators who can offer thoughtful, constructive feedback that helps you grow as an artist.

Responding with Grace and Gratitude

When faced with criticism, respond with grace and gratitude. Instead of becoming defensive or dismissive, listen carefully to what is being said and consider how you can use the feedback to improve your work. Express gratitude to those who take the time to offer constructive criticism, acknowledging their efforts to help you grow as an artist.

Turning Criticism into Fuel for Growth

Finally, learn to harness the power of criticism as fuel for growth. Instead of allowing negative feedback to discourage you, use it as motivation

to push yourself further, to experiment boldly, and to strive for excellence in your work. Remember that every critique, no matter how harsh, is an opportunity to learn and grow as an artist.

Conclusion

Navigating criticism with confidence is an essential skill for any artist. By embracing a growth mindset, separating the art from the artist, seeking out constructive feedback, responding with grace and gratitude, and turning criticism into fuel for growth, you can transform even the most challenging feedback into an opportunity for artistic development. So embrace criticism as a vital part of your artistic journey, and let it propel you toward ever-greater heights of creativity and excellence.

CHAPTER 7: THE ART OF RISK-TAKING

In the realm of artistry, risk-taking is not just a choice—it's a necessity. It's the willingness to venture into uncharted territory, to push beyond the boundaries of comfort and convention, and to embrace the unknown with courage and conviction. In this chapter, we'll explore the art of risk-taking and discover how daring to step outside of your comfort zone can lead to breakthroughs in creativity and innovation.

Embracing Uncertainty

At the heart of risk-taking lies uncertainty—the fear of the unknown, the possibility of failure, and the allure of the unexplored. Yet, it is in embracing uncertainty that true growth and discovery often occur. By stepping outside of your comfort zone and venturing into the unknown, you open yourself up to new possibilities, new perspectives, and new experiences that can enrich your artistic journey in profound and unexpected ways.

Pushing Beyond Comfort

Risk-taking requires courage—the courage to push beyond the boundaries of comfort and fa

miliarity and to confront the fears and doubts that hold you back. It's about challenging yourself to go beyond what is safe and predictable, to embrace the discomfort of the unknown, and to trust in your own ability to navigate the challenges that lie ahead. By pushing beyond your comfort zone, you expand your creative horizons and unlock new depths of potential within yourself.

Embracing Failure as Growth

In the pursuit of artistic excellence, failure is not a setback—it's a stepping stone on the path to success. Risk-taking inevitably involves the possibility of failure, but it is through failure that we learn, grow, and evolve as artists. By embracing failure as an essential part of the creative process, you can free yourself from the fear of making mistakes and open yourself up to new opportunities for learning and growth.

Cultivating Resilience

Risk-taking requires resilience—the ability to bounce back from setbacks, to persevere in the face of adversity, and to maintain unwavering faith in your creative vision. It's about cultivating a mindset of resilience that allows you to weather the inevitable challenges and setbacks that come with taking risks. By developing resilience, you can navigate the ups and downs of the creative process with grace and fortitude, emerging stronger and more resilient with each new challenge you encounter.

Celebrating Boldness and Innovation

Ultimately, risk-taking is about celebrating boldness and innovation—the willingness to defy conventions, challenge the status quo, and push the boundaries of what is possible. It's about embracing the thrill of the unknown, the excitement of exploration, and the joy of discovery that comes with daring to take risks. By embracing risk-

taking as an integral part of your artistic practice, you can unlock new levels of creativity, innovation, and inspiration that have the power to transform not only your art but also the world around you.

Conclusion

The art of risk-taking is not for the faint of heart—it requires courage, resilience, and a willingness to embrace uncertainty. But it is through risk-taking that true breakthroughs in creativity and innovation often occur. So dare to venture into the unknown, to push beyond the boundaries of comfort and convention, and to embrace the exhilarating journey of risk-taking. For it is in tak

ing risks that we truly discover what it means to be an artist.

CHAPTER 8: CULTIVATING A UNIQUE ARTISTIC VOICE

Your artistic voice is the essence of who you are as a creator—it's what sets your work apart and makes it unmistakably yours. In this chapter, we'll explore the importance of cultivating a unique artistic voice and discover strategies for uncovering and expressing your true creative identity.

Embracing Authenticity

At the core of cultivating a unique artistic voice lies authenticity— the courage to be true to yourself, your experiences, and your perspective. It's about embracing your quirks, flaws, and idiosyncrasies, and allowing them to shine through in your work. By embracing authenticity, you can tap into the raw, unfiltered essence of your creativity and create art that resonates with genuine emotion and sincerity.

Reflecting on Personal Experience

Your artistic voice is deeply intertwined with your personal experiences, beliefs, and values. Take the time to reflect on your life journey, your cultural heritage, and the moments that have shaped you as a person. Draw inspiration from your own ex

periences and use them as fuel for your creative expression. By infusing your work with personal meaning and authenticity, you can create art that is truly unique to you.

Experimenting with Style and Technique

Cultivating a unique artistic voice often involves experimentation— exploring different styles, techniques, and mediums until you find what resonates most deeply with you. Don't be afraid to push the boundaries of your creativity, to try new things, and to embrace the unknown. By experimenting with style and technique, you can uncover hidden depths of your artistic identity and discover new avenues for creative expression.

Finding Your Signature Themes

Every artist has their own signature themes— the recurring motifs, symbols, and subjects that appear throughout their work. Take the time to identify the themes that resonate most deeply with you and explore them in depth. Whether it's exploring the beauty of nature, delving into the complexities of the human experience, or grappling with existential questions, finding your signature themes can help you cultivate a unique artistic voice that is distinctly yours.

Listening to Your Intuition

Above all, cultivating a unique artistic voice requires listening to your intuition— the inner voice that guides you towards your true creative identity. Trust your instincts, follow your passions, and allow your intuition to lead you towards the art that feels most authentic to you. By listening to your intuition, you can tap into the wellspring of creativity within you and create art that is truly reflective of your unique artistic voice.

Conclusion

Cultivating a unique artistic voice is a deeply personal journey—one that requires courage, introspection, and a willingness to embrace authenticity. By embracing authenticity, reflecting on personal experience, experimenting with style and technique, finding your signature themes, and listening to your intuition, you can uncover the true essence of your creativity and create art that is unmistakably yours. So embrace the journey of self-discovery, and let your unique artistic voice shine bright for the world to see.

CHAPTER 9: HONING YOUR CRAFT WITH PASSION AND PERSISTENCE

Mastering your craft is a journey of dedication, fuelled by passion and sustained by unwavering persistence. In this chapter, we'll delve into the importance of honing your craft with fervent enthusiasm and relentless perseverance, exploring strategies for continuous improvement and growth as an artist.

Cultivating Passion

Passion is the driving force behind mastery—it's what fuels your creativity, ignites your inspiration, and propels you forward on your artistic journey. Cultivate a deep-seated passion for your craft, nurturing it with curiosity, enthusiasm, and a thirst for knowledge. Let your passion infuse every brushstroke, every note, and every word, imbuing your work with a sense of vitality and vitality that is truly infectious.

Embracing the Learning Process

Honing your craft is an ongoing process of learning and growth, marked by experimentation, exploration, and discovery. Embrace the learning process with an open mind and a willingness to push beyond your comfort zone. Seek out opportunities for education and mentorship, immerse yourself in new experiences, and never stop striving for improvement. By embracing the learning process, you can continually expand your skills and deepen your understanding of your craft.

Setting Goals and Pursuing Excellence

Set ambitious goals for yourself and pursue excellence with unwavering determination. Define clear, actionable objectives that align with your artistic vision and commit yourself wholeheartedly to achieving them. Break down your goals into manageable steps, track your progress diligently, and celebrate your successes along the way. By setting goals and pursuing excellence, you can push yourself to new heights of creativity and achievement.

Embracing Failure as Growth

Failure is an inevitable part of the creative process, but it is also a powerful teacher. Embrace failure as an opportunity for growth, learning, and self-discovery. Instead of allowing setbacks to discourage you, use them as motivation to push harder, to try new approaches, and to refine your skills. By embracing failure as an essential part of your journey, you can develop resilience, grit, and a deep sense of self-confidence that will serve you well in all aspects of your life.

Cultivating a Growth Mindset

Cultivate a growth mindset—a belief in your ability to learn, adapt, and improve over time. Approach challenges with optimism and curiosity, viewing them as opportunities for growth and development rather than obstacles to be overcome. Foster a spirit of resilience, flexibility, and adaptability, and embrace the inevitable ups and downs of your artistic journey with grace and determination. By cultivating a growth mindset, you can unlock your full potential as an artist and achieve mastery in your craft.

Conclusion

Honing your craft with passion and persistence is a journey of dedication, fuelled by a deep-seated love for your art and a relentless commitment to excellence. By cultivating passion, embracing the learning process, setting goals, embracing failure as growth, and cultivating a growth mindset, you can continually push yourself to new heights of creativity and achievement. So, embrace the journey of mastery, and let your passion and persistence propel you towards greatness in your craft.

CHAPTER 10: BALANCING TRADITION WITH INNOVATION

Finding the delicate balance between tradition and innovation is a challenge faced by many artists. In this chapter, we'll explore the importance of honouring artistic traditions while embracing innovation, and discover how blending the old with the new can lead to truly groundbreaking creative endeavours.

Respecting Artistic Heritage

Tradition is the foundation upon which artistic innovation is built—it's the wisdom passed down through generations, the techniques perfected over centuries, and the cultural heritage that informs our creative identity. Respect and honour artistic traditions, acknowledging the contributions of those who came before us and the rich tapestry of history that shapes our craft.

Embracing the Spirit of Innovation

Innovation is the lifeblood of creativity—it's the driving force that propels art forward, pushing the boundaries of what is possible and challenging us to see the world in new ways. Embrace the spirit of innovation, daring to experiment with new techniques, explore uncharted territory, and defy conventions in pursuit of your artistic vision.

Finding Harmony Between Old and New

Balancing tradition with innovation requires finding harmony between the old and the new—blending time-

honoured techniques with cutting-edge ideas to create something truly unique. Draw inspiration from the past while looking towards the future, weaving together elements of tradition and innovation to create art that is both timeless and relevant to the modern world.

Pushing Boundaries Without Losing Sight of Roots

Pushing boundaries is essential for artistic growth, but it's important not to lose sight of your artistic roots in the process. Stay grounded in your artistic heritage, drawing strength and inspiration from the traditions that have shaped your craft. Push boundaries with purpose and intention, always mindful of the rich artistic legacy that informs your work.

Fostering Dialogue Between Past and Present

Foster a dialogue between past and present, inviting tradition and innovation to converse and collaborate in the creative process. Learn from the wisdom of the past while embracing the possibilities of the future, allowing the exchange of ideas to enrich and invigorate your artistic practice.

Conclusion

Balancing tradition with innovation is a delicate dance—one that requires reverence for the past and a bold vision for the future. By respecting artistic heritage, embracing the spirit of innovation, finding harmony between old and new, pushing boundaries without losing sight of roots, and fostering dialogue between past and present, you can create art that honours the traditions of the past while paving the way for the artistic innovations of tomorrow.

CHAPTER 11: CREATING IMPACTFUL ART THAT CHALLENGES THE STATUS QUO

Art has the power to challenge, provoke, and inspire change. In this chapter, we'll explore the importance of creating impactful art that challenges the status quo, and discover how artists can use their creative voice to spark meaningful dialogue and drive social change.

Art as a Catalyst for Change

Art has long been a powerful tool for challenging the status quo and advocating for social change. Whether through visual art, music, literature, or performance, artists have the ability to shine a light on injustice, amplify marginalized voices, and inspire action towards a more just and equitable society.

Sparking Dialogue and Debate

Impactful art challenges the status quo by sparking dialogue and debate, encouraging viewers to question their assumptions, confront uncomfortable truths, and consider alternative perspectives. By provoking thought and fostering empathy, artists can inspire meaningful conversations that lead to greater understanding and social change.

Amplifying Marginalized Voices

One of the most powerful ways art can challenge the status quo is by amplifying the voices of those who have been marginalized or silenced by society. Through storytelling, representation, and advocacy, artists can give voice to the voiceless, shining a spotlight on issues of injustice and inequality and driving awareness and action towards positive change.

Advocating for Social Justice

Artists have a unique platform to advocate for social justice and human rights, using their creative talents to raise awareness of pressing issues and mobilize communities for action. Whether through public art installations, protest songs, or performance art, artists can leverage their platform to advocate for a more just, equitable, and inclusive world.

Empowering Others to Speak Out

Impactful art not only challenges the status quo—it empowers others to speak out and take action for change. By sharing their stories, expressing their truths, and standing up for what they believe in, artists can inspire others to find their

own voice and join the fight for social justice and equality.

Conclusion

Creating impactful art that challenges the status quo is a powerful act of courage, compassion, and creativity. By sparking dialogue and debate, amplifying marginalized voices, advocating for social justice, and empowering others to speak out, artists can use their creative talents to drive meaningful change in the world. So let your art be a force for good, and let your voice be heard in the fight for a brighter, more just future.

CHAPTER 12: OVERCOMING CREATIVE BLOCKS WITH REBELLION

Creative blocks are an inevitable part of the artistic process, but they don't have to be a roadblock. In this chapter, we'll explore how rebellion can be a powerful tool for overcoming creative blocks, unlocking new levels of creativity, and unleashing the full potential of your artistic vision.

Embracing Creative Rebellion

Creative rebellion is about defying the constraints of convention and breaking free from the limitations of your own mind. It's about daring to challenge the status quo, push beyond your comfort zone, and embrace the unknown with courage and conviction. By embracing creative rebellion, you can unlock new levels of creativity and push past the barriers that stand in the way of your artistic vision.

Embracing Chaos and Uncertainty

Creative blocks often stem from a fear of failure, a fear of the unknown, or a fear of not being good enough. By embracing chaos and uncertainty, you can learn to see these fears not as obstacles, but as opportunities for growth and exploration. Embrace the messiness of the creative process, the

unpredictability of inspiration, and the thrill of venturing into uncharted territory. By embracing chaos and uncertainty, you can free yourself from the grip of creative blocks and unleash your full creative potential.

Breaking Free from Routine and Convention

Creative blocks can also be the result of falling into a rut or sticking too closely to routine and convention. Break free from the constraints of your comfort zone, shake up your routine, and dare to try something new. Whether it's experimenting with a different medium, exploring a new subject matter, or collaborating with other artists, breaking free from routine and convention can breathe new life into your creative practice and reignite your passion for making art.

Trusting Your Instincts

Above all, overcoming creative blocks with rebellion requires trusting your instincts and listening to your inner voice. Trust that you have the knowledge, the skills, and the creativity to overcome any obstacle that stands in your way. Trust that inspiration will come when you least expect it, and that the answers you seek are already within you. By trusting your instincts, you can tap into the wellspring of creativity within you and unlock new levels of artistic brilliance.

Conclusion

Creative blocks are a natural part of the artistic process, but they don't have to hold you back. By embracing creative rebellion, embracing chaos and uncertainty, breaking free from routine and convention, and trusting your instincts, you can overcome creative blocks and unlock new levels of creativity and inspiration. So, *embrace the rebellious spirit within you, and let it propel you towards artistic greatness.*

CHAPTER 13: BUILDING A COMMUNITY OF FELLOW REBELS

In the journey of artistic rebellion, there is strength in numbers. In this chapter, we'll explore the importance of building a community of fellow rebels—like-minded individuals who share your passion for pushing boundaries, challenging conventions, and creating art that defies expectations.

Finding Your Tribe

Building a community of fellow rebels starts with finding your tribe—the people who share your values, your vision, and your commitment to artistic rebellion. Seek out like-minded individuals through local art collectives, online forums, and social media groups, and cultivate meaningful connections with those who inspire and support your creative journey.

Fostering Collaboration and Connection

Once you've found your tribe, foster collaboration and connection by engaging in meaningful dialogue, sharing ideas and resources, and collaborating on creative projects. By working together with fellow rebels, you can amplify your impact, explore new perspectives, and push the boundaries of your creativity in ways you never thought possible.

Offering Support and Encouragement

Building a community of fellow rebels isn't just about what you can get—it's also about what you can give.

Offer support and encouragement to your fellow artists, celebrating their successes, offering constructive feedback, and lending a helping hand when they need it most. By fostering a culture of support and camaraderie, you can create a community that uplifts and inspires everyone within it.

Challenging Each Other to Grow

A community of fellow rebels isn't afraid to challenge each other to grow. Encourage your fellow artists to push beyond their comfort zones, explore new ideas, and take risks in their creative practice. By challenging each other to grow, you can inspire one another to reach new heights of artistic excellence and innovation.

Celebrating Diversity and Inclusion

Finally, a community of fellow rebels celebrates diversity and inclusion, recognizing that true creativity thrives on the rich tapestry of human experience. Embrace artists from all walks of life, regardless of race, gender, sexuality, or background, and create a space where everyone feels welcome, valued, and empowered to express their unique voice.

Conclusion

Building a community of fellow rebels is essential for any artist who seeks to challenge the status quo and make a lasting impact with their work. By finding your tribe, fostering collaboration and connection, offering support and encouragement, challenging each other to grow, and celebrating diversity and inclusion, you can create a community that empowers everyone within it to embrace their rebellious spirit and create art that truly matters.

CHAPTER 14: EMBRACING CHANGE AND ADAPTATION

Change is inevitable in the ever-evolving landscape of artistry, but it doesn't have to be feared. In this chapter, we'll explore the importance of embracing change and adaptation as an artist, and discover strategies for navigating the shifting tides of creativity with grace and resilience.

Embracing the Fluidity of Creativity

Creativity is a fluid, ever-changing force that defies definition and resists confinement. Embrace the fluidity of creativity, allowing yourself to flow with the changing currents of inspiration and intuition. Be open to new ideas, new influences, and new ways of thinking, and embrace change as a natural and necessary part of the creative process.

Navigating Uncertainty with Grace

Change often brings uncertainty, but it's important not to let fear hold you back. Instead, navigate uncertainty with grace and resilience, trusting in your ability to adapt and thrive in the face of adversity. Stay flexible and open-minded, embracing the unknown with curiosity and courage, and allow yourself to grow and evolve with each new challenge you encounter.

Learning from Failure and Setbacks

Failure and setbacks are inevitable on the path of artistic growth, but they are also powerful teachers. Embrace failure as an opportunity for learning and growth, rather than a sign of defeat. Reflect on your mistakes, extract valuable lessons from your experiences, and use them to inform your future creative endeavours. By learning from failure and setbacks, you can transform adversity into opportunity and emerge stronger and more resilient than ever before.

Embracing Innovation and Experimentation

Change often brings opportunities for innovation and experimentation, so embrace them with enthusiasm and curiosity. Be willing to try new things, explore new ideas, and push the boundaries of your creativity in pursuit of your artistic vision. Embrace failure as a natural part of the creative process, and allow yourself the freedom to take risks and explore uncharted territory.

Cultivating Resilience and Adaptability

Above all, embracing change and adaptation requires cultivating resilience and adaptability—the ability to bounce back from setbacks, to pivot in response to new challenges, and to thrive in the face of uncertainty. Cultivate a mindset of resilience, flexibility, and perseverance, and trust in your ability to weather the storms of change with grace and courage.

Conclusion

Change is inevitable in the world of artistry, but it doesn't have to be feared. By embracing change and adaptation as natural and necessary parts of the creative process, you can navigate the shifting tides of creativity with grace, resilience, and courage. So, embrace the unknown, trust in your ability to adapt and thrive, and allow yourself to grow and evolve with each new challenge you encounter.

CHAPTER 15: MAKING YOUR ART MATTER: ADVOCACY AND ACTIVISM

Art has the power to inspire change, challenge perceptions, and amplify voices that have been silenced. In this chapter, we'll explore the importance of using your artistic platform for advocacy and activism, and discover how artists can harness their creative talents to make a meaningful impact on the world around them.

Using Art as a Tool for Change

Art has a unique ability to transcend language, culture, and ideology, reaching people on a deeply emotional and visceral level. Use your art as a tool for change, shining a spotlight on pressing social issues, raising awareness of injustice and inequality, and inspiring others to take action for positive change.

Amplifying Marginalized Voices

One of the most powerful ways artists can advocate for change is by amplifying the voices of those who have been marginalized or silenced by society. Use your platform to give voice to the voiceless, sharing their stories, experiences, and perspectives with the world. By amplifying marginalized voices, you can challenge systemic oppression and work towards a more just and equitable society.

Sparking Dialogue and Empathy

Art has the power to spark dialogue, foster empathy, and bridge the divides that separate us. Use your art to start conversations, provoke thought, and encourage viewers to see the world from different perspectives. By fostering empathy and understanding, you can build bridges between communities, break down barriers, and pave the way for meaningful social change.

Advocating for Human Rights and Social Justice

Artists have a unique platform to advocate for human rights and social justice, using their creative talents to raise awareness of pressing issues and mobilize communities for action. Whether through public art installations, protest songs, or performance art, artists can leverage their platform to shine a light on injustice and inspire others to stand up for what is right.

Empowering Others to Make a Difference

Above all, use your art to empower others to make a difference. Inspire and mobilize your audience to take action for positive change, whether it's through volunteering, activism, or advocacy. By harnessing the power of collective action, you can amplify your impact and create lasting change that reverberates far beyond the confines of the art world.

Conclusion

Making your art matter means using your creative talents to advocate for change, challenge injustice, and inspire others to make a difference. By using art as a tool for change, amplifying marginalized voices, sparking dialogue and empathy, advocating for human rights and social justice, and empowering others to make a difference, you can harness the full power of your artistic platform to create a more just, equitable, and compassionate world. So let your art be a force for good, and let your voice be heard in the fight for a brighter, more hopeful future.

CONCLUSION: EMBRACING YOUR REBEL ARTISTRY JOURNEY

Congratulations on completing your journey of rebel artistry! Throughout this book, we've explored the importance of authenticity, creativity, and courage in cultivating your unique artistic voice, challenging the status quo, and making a meaningful impact with your art. From embracing imperfection to navigating criticism, from pushing boundaries to building a community of fellow rebels, you've embarked on a transformative journey of self-discovery and creative exploration.

As you continue on your rebel artistry journey, remember to stay true to yourself, embrace change and adaptation, and use your artistic platform to advocate for change and inspire others. Your voice is powerful, your vision is unique, and your art has the potential to make a lasting impact on the world around you.

Embrace your rebel spirit, trust in your creative instincts, and never be afraid to push the boundaries of what is possible. Your journey as an artist is just beginning, and the possibilities are endless.

ACKNOWLEDGMENTS

I would like to express my deepest gratitude to all those who have supported me on my journey of rebel artistry. To my mentors, collaborators, and fellow artists who have inspired and encouraged me along the way, thank you for believing in me and pushing me to strive for excellence. To my friends and family who have stood by me through the highs and lows, thank you for your unwavering love and support. And to the readers of this book, thank you for joining me on this journey of creativity, rebellion, and self-discovery. May your own rebel artistry journey be filled with passion, courage, and boundless creativity.

ABOUT THE AUTHOR

Godfrey Serene is a multi-talented individual with a deep passion for art, creativity, and technology. As an artist and painter, he brings his vivid imagination to life on canvas, exploring themes of beauty, mystery, and wonder in his work. With a keen eye for detail and a love for experimentation, Godfrey's art captivates audiences and invites them into his richly imagined worlds.

In addition to his visual artistry, Godfrey is also a creative author, weaving tales of adventure, romance, and intrigue in his fiction novels. His storytelling prowess transports readers to fantastical realms where anything is possible, sparking their imagination and igniting their sense of wonder.

Beyond his pursuits in the arts, Godfrey is also an AI prompt engineer, leveraging his expertise in computer science to push the boundaries of creativity and innovation. His work in artificial intelligence explores the intersection of technology and art, offering new possibilities for creative expression and exploration.

As a Microsoft certified professional, Godfrey brings a wealth of technical knowledge and expertise to his creative endeavours, ensuring that his artistic vision is realized with precision and skill. His dedication to his craft and his commitment to excellence are evident in everything he does, from his stunning artworks to his captivating novels to his ground-breaking work in AI.

Godfrey is an omnist who believes in the power of art to transcend boundaries, unite humanity, and inspire positive change. He approaches his work with a spirit of openness, curiosity, and unconditional love, embracing the beauty of diversity and celebrating the infinite possibilities of the creative imagination.

In all of his pursuits, Godfrey seeks to inspire others to embrace their own creativity, follow their passions, and pursue their dreams with courage and conviction. With a boundless enthusiasm for art and a deep reverence for the creative process, he continues to push the boundaries of what is possible, leaving an indelible mark on the world of art and technology alike.

www.ingramcontent.com/pod-product-compliance
Lightning Source LLC
Chambersburg PA
CBHW030514220526
45464CB00006B/2793